DOGGOS

A to Z

A pithy guide to 26 dog breeds.

Original rhymes and watercolor illustrations
by Heather Kent

Dedicated to my three dear human puppers:
Abel, Olive, & Fern

A

Afghan Hound

An Afghan Hound's soft
Not unlike a small blanket,
With fur that's so long
You can braid (but dont yank!) it.

B Bull Terrier

A Bull Terrier's a clown
Whose best friend is a man,
And she'll do as you bid
(If it's already her plan).

C Corgi

C is for Corgi,
She's Queen of the Yappy.
She's short on her legs
But not short on her happy.

D Dachshund

A Doxie (or Wiener)
Is as loyal as long,
But mom does get mad
When he pees on her thongs.

E English Springer Spaniel

Whether he is black and white
Or is he white and brown,
This English Spaniel with curled ears
Loves springing up and down.

F

French Bulldog

French Bulldogs (so cute!)
Are lazy as can be.
But that's OK,
I like my friends to be the same as me.

G

Greyhound

They have happy long faces
And eyes of a doe,
Greyhounds are the gentlest
Racers I know.

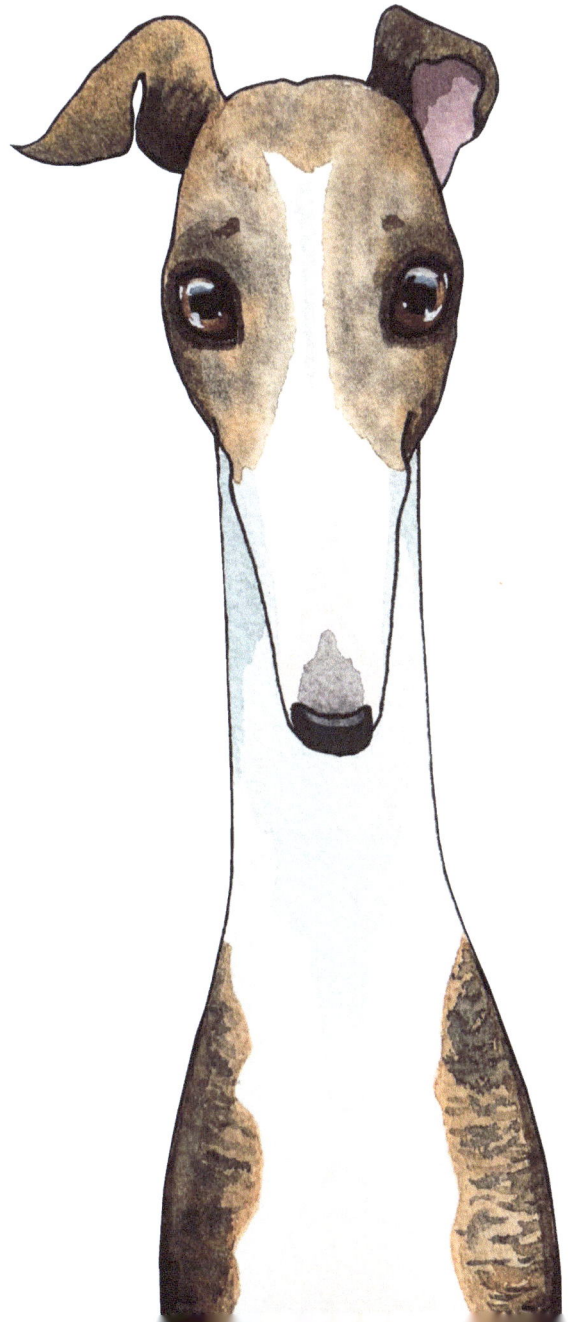

H Harrier

Few breeds to the rabbit are
Scarier
Than the hunter (though kid-friendly!)
Harrier.

I Irish Setter

Irish Setters are redheads
With questionable smarts,
But they sure compensate
With their big hippie hearts.

J

Jindo

Though a Jindo is aloof
And he thinks you should submit to him,
He'll love you without woof
If you just don't make him go to swim.

K King Charles Spaniel

The King Charles Spaniel is
Happy and mellow;
He's always a cheerfully
Biddable fellow.

L Labrador

Yellow, Black or Chocolate,
I am willing to bet
Your Lab's more like a brother
Than he is like a pet.

M Mutt

A mixed breed, or mongrel,
Or hybrid, or mutt
Will still love you always,
No matter the what.

N Newfoundland

A Newfie's a bear
Who's not grizzly or cruel,
If a bear's a large lapdog
Who is swimming
[in drool].

O Old English Sheepdog

The best kind of Sheepdog
Is English and Old.
She likes herding children
As well as her fold.

P

Pug

I love a stout dog
With a round but flat mug.
My favorite might be
The awake-snoring Pug.

Q

Queensland Heeler

Q is for Queensland,
She's not from New Zealand.
"Heeler?" You wonder?
Cattle Dog from Down Under.

R Rhodesian Ridgeback

Dogs love chasing cats,
It is kind of cliché,
But Ridgebacks were bred
To chase LIONS away.

S

Shiba Inu

If you adopt a Shiba Inu
(With a smile just as sly as can be)
You'll oft be saying, "He's not a fox,
He's a Spitz who's more clever than me."

T Tibetan Terrier

This by-name-only Terrier
In Tibet was first bred
To be gifts from the monks,
The old legends have said.

U Utonagan

Utonagan's a dog
Though a wolf he looks like,
He doesn't eat grandmas
Or men on a hike.

V

Vizsla

These self-grooming Vizslas
Are copper in hue;
Their eyes match their fur,
And their noses do too.

W

West Highland White Terrier

Westies have tails that are strong
And are sturdy,
For pulling them out when they're stuck
In deep dirt-y.

X

Xoloitzcuintli

X is for Xolo,
A smooth Suavecito.
He was born with no coat,
But he needs no tuxedo.

Y

Yorkshire Terrier

Yorkies are teacup,
But rodents they'll fight.
What they're lacking in size
They make up for in might.

Z Zuchon

Zuchon might just be
The only breed beginning
With the letter Z.

www.ingramcontent.com/pod-product-compliance
Lightning Source LLC
Chambersburg PA
CBHW042026090426

42811CB00016B/1755